MW00945118

WHEN THREADS WEAR THIN

Soul Stirrings of an Octogenarian

By Sister Carol Ann Collins, SSND

Dedicated to:

My family, friends and School Sisters of Notre Dame, who have loved me, touched and molded me—smoothed . . . and suffered from . . . and helped me reform the rough edges of my being.

Sister Carol Ann Collins, SSND
Spring, 2019

Acknowledgement

Neither the hand-written word nor computer file can adequately express my heartfelt gratitude to and for my dear friend—

~ Vicky Meehan ~

—who has been guide, counselor, editor, trainer, conscience, support, and more throughout the creation of this book.

TABLE OF CONTENTS

Foreword

addressing my potential audience
and setting out my purpose

Until I officially retired at age 82, I was too busy—scheduling, planning, travelling from place to place—to notice my octogenarian body, mind and spirit beginning to morph into a new kind of being. As the subsequent years, months, days continue to unfold without someone else's schedule determining mine, my awareness of significant changes in how I think, sleep and move keeps growing sharper. I have time and space now not only to discover, but also to record in writing, details of my late-in-life journey. I don't recall anyone ever teaching me (or even suggesting how) to behold, hold onto, and cherish such important lessons that I am learning throughout these unique twilight years of my life.

I sense an inner calling and impelling desire to write the story of what I am learning now (in my 80's) and to offer my personal reflections as a legacy to the living members of my hereditary family and close friends, including the School Sisters of Notre Dame, all of whom have touched and molded me with their presence, their influence, their challenges.

While the text I create here is taking on the form of a "book," its contents are not specifically intended to be read cover to cover. My desire is to present a smorgasbord of reflective essays on the human experiences of an aging person. The table of contents serves as a compass, pointing to specific late-life issues and lessons learned as events and scenarios continue to become my personal life's "last chapter" classroom. An appendix of suggested reflection questions on each chapter provides opportunity for you to contemplate your own life in relationship to growing older.

A *readers' alert* seems appropriate here. The content of my text includes little, if anything, of my childhood, adolescence, and early adulthood. I acknowledge that my readers may, now and then, be curious to know more about my earlier years. My concentration in this writing, however, rests primarily on my personal experience of being 80-plus years old, moving into my 90's, and preparing for my final life in time here on earth. Besides, so much of my younger existence has already faded in my memory . . . threads not only thinned but vanished completely from my mind.

As I wobbled through life's events this past octogenarian decade, new realizations, discoveries, and even some fresh convictions have now become a guide for my daily living. I so often found myself saying, over and over, I wish someone had told me that this is how the later years *could* be, and more and more often, how they *would* be.

I believe and hope the learnings that have now embedded themselves into my daily living may be of help to others as they wend their own way through life's journey and the process of growing old and older. Perhaps, too, my sharing may prompt an idea to help someone traverse more-than-a-few possible vexing hours of troublesome days.

The sub-title and much of this work's content (which I often refer to as "my book") borders on what some might call *theological reflection*. I don't seek here, nor make claim to, any theological expertise. What I write does not stem from any forever-fixed belief of mine but is, rather, a set of wonderments—musings I present as propositions—gleaned from my own prayer, reflections on Scripture, and resulting from daily grace received.

My personal desire and goal for writing this material is to pass on to my family and other companions-on-the-journey some of my personal experience and realizations about living through being 80 years old, leaning towards 90, and knowing that the moment we humans call *death* is looming ever-closer.

Among educators and others, there is a popular cliché: "*When the student is ready, the teacher will appear.*" Thus it happened for me that during my early ruminations about aging, three books by Kathleen Dowling Singh came to my attention and eventual possession. Her books, The Grace of Dying

(1998); <u>The Grace of Aging</u> (2014); and <u>Unbinding</u> (2017) are, indeed, a treasure-trove of ideas, reflections and serious challenges for those of us reaching beyond our 80th birthdays. The readers of this book, <u>When Threads Wear Thin</u>, will find frequent reference to Singh's passages.

Singh writes from her own Buddhist tradition, yet artistically blends Buddhist ideals with Christianity, especially regarding the practice of mindfulness and centering prayer. Singh frequently quotes Christian writers and believers such as Thomas Merton and Richard Rohr. Her books are reference-worthy resources as we wonder through our late-in-life years.

I
Thinning of Threads and Starkness of Holes

slowly growing awareness of how life
as I have known it is slipping away and
how I might tend to "holes" that confront me

I had just taken off my shoes and climbed up onto the chiropractor's table. As I turned over, I noticed a large, gaping hole in the right heel of my bright red sock. As the sight of the tear registered, I immediately felt both shock and embarrassment. After all, I had taken special care to choose these socks to match my new outfit. Alas, my careful planning had gone amiss. At the same instant, my grandmother's voice from the past echoed these words in my head: "NEVER wear torn or soiled clothing when you are going to the doctor." Fortunately, such thoughts lasted but a fleeting moment.

The chiropractic visit became more than a rearrangement my spine's sinews. Later, my "discovery of the sock hole without having previously noticed the thinning threads" incident presented itself as an invitation and passport to a spiritual quest. What lessons, might I uncover from the image of the sock and its hole?

1

Some days after the hole-in-the-sock event, in the midst of my morning prayer time, that torn stocking image came back to mind. Over the years, I had developed a habit of ear-marking such haphazard events that seemed to leave a wrinkle in my memory and using them as a springboard for a set of new life-learnings. A friend of mine had given me a special term for these unexpected realizations. He called them *teach-ments.*

What follows here are some very important *teach-ments* about threads—some so sublime as to reform religious beliefs—some as simple as making a change in how I plan my day. These are threads that (each in its own way) serve to hold me together, day by day. And now, in the later years of my life, I find myself wanting to become *more* conscientious about the condition of threads I hold dear, while learning to fret *less* about threads that matter little. Somehow, my mental picture of the hole-in-the-sock has become a well-spring of significant realizations for me, all related to my aging-process experience and how to deal with so-called end-of-life issues.

Too often, I give only fleeting attention to life passing me by. I had not noticed, at all, the threads wearing thin at the heel point of my socks—much like the many other threads wearing thin in my octogenarian life. There are those long-term friendships accompanied by phone calls and mailings that appear less frequently. My list of professional appointments seems a thing of the past, and invitations for speaking engagements come maybe once a year, if at all. Social dates on my calendar have given way, instead, to necessary appointments with a growing variety of health-care professionals. In hindsight, I can see such changes did, indeed, develop gradually and imperceptibly.

Over time, as I continued to reflect on threads thinning and my surprise at holes unexpectedly appearing, I sensed a poem creating itself in my mind:

Life's Diminishments

As threads wear thin,
a hole is on its way
into its own being.
Suddenly, it's there,
—an unexpected,
sometimes embarrassing,
and more often, a frightening
void . . .
a bold space of nothing,
where I had expected
something to be and to remain.

My poem well describes, I believe, what I mean by the word "holes" used to portray the void I experience when something of great value to my sense of well-being has disappeared. Even as I write this text, I continue to ponder life's phenomenon of how, too frequently, I become so comfortable I forget that not only are the seasons of the year changing, but so am I. As are *all* those whom I know.

Professional Identity

I was, undeniably, comfortable with the way life picked up and continued to unfold in 1999, once my second term in administration of my religious order ended. When I was unexpectedly elected to leadership in 1991, I had been able to set aside my consultant/facilitator career for a while, not unlike slipping stitches to an extra knitting needle where they would wait until I wanted to pick them up again to continue my knitting pattern.

So it was, that in 1999 at the close of my administrative term, I continued my career as facilitator/consultant and spiritual advisor. I gave scant notice to the fact I was now eight years older. A lot of travelling was involved. No matter! While in administration, I had travelled to Africa, Italy, Canada and across the USA.

Then in 2009, I was invited to create and conduct an eight-day retreat. Subject matter consisted of Alcoholics Anonymous' Twelve Steps and the official Constitution of the School Sisters of Notre Dame (129 pages) which describes the life-style and practices of my religious order's members. I surmised that designing such a retreat could be a formidable task, yet I felt quite privileged to be considered for this project. It surely boosted my self-image to know someone recognized and valued my abilities.

I did take some time to ponder what my response to this arduous invitation might be. I remember sensing that if I were able to devise such a retreat, ramifications of the retreat's content might reach more than a few School Sisters of Notre Dame who were currently suffering the dreadful effects of addiction. I came to believe God was moving me, gradually and gently, to accept the invitation and to take on the task of constructing such a program, so I said yes to the invitation.

Over the next seven months (I was now past age 80!), I meditated, read, reflected, prayed, consulted, and managed to write eight conference talks along with a 37-page reflection booklet.

My mind was working non-stop between September, 2009 and April, 2010. All through those months, I vacillated between (a) feeling truly spirit-led as I wrote or (b) regular weariness by my own question, *"Why in the world did I agree to be part of this project?"* Yet, each and every day, words and ideas kept stirring in my mind, spilling out onto the word processor. My very good friend, Vicky, had offered to help with editing and formatting my work. She was always there in the background encouraging me forward. God surely had a direct part in providing everything I needed to generate the retreat content.

Now as I look back, I don't recall ever giving thought during those busy, busy months to the fact that I was sorely taxing body, mind, and spirit. Regretfully, I no longer have among my personal possessions the spiritual journal of those months back in 2009-10. I have to rely solely on my memory of that time. I am wondering if I ever gave attention during those work-soaked months to the over-all toll on my being. I do remember how exhaustion became a daily part of my preparation work; and how relieved I was when the program talks were down on paper, the reflection booklet printed, collated, and sent on (in advance) to the Guest House Retreat Center in Lake Orion, Michigan where the retreat would be conducted.

Some dozen School Sisters of Notre Dame, who were participating in the retreat, kept showering me with words of gratitude all throughout the eight days. Following the retreat, I had time to visit briefly with friends in Detroit before heading back to St. Louis. I could rest, then, in the knowledge that both God and the retreatants were saying to me, "Thanks for a job well done!"

Only sometime after my return from Michigan did I begin to realize that I was, indeed, getting older! In retrospect, I do not believe that any kind of negativity or "hole" in my self-image was beginning to form.

But I did come to note that my time-tried sources of renewing energy were themselves wearing thin. Thus it was that after the retreat at Guest House, I made the decision to take on no more requests for retreats. Several months later, I announced my official retirement from offering spiritual direction by appointment.

To fill the holes in my calendar, I began designing an outline for the book you now hold in your hand. From time to time, given certain circumstances, the question does arise in my mind, *"Did I retire too soon?"*

Now that I am, in memory, seriously rewinding the tape of those tiring months prior to the Guest House retreat and reconsidering the impact on and response of the retreat participants, I can now declare to myself and to you, the reader, that the retreat design and content was and is one of the most significant service ministries of my religious life. I believe that my God concurs.

I am beginning to realize that the written content of that retreat and this very book are two concrete ways which evidence my personal contribution to the world. I know, of course, that many individuals were earlier-influenced by my years as a school teacher, etc. Yet, their thoughts and remembrances of me and what they learned (or did not learn) from me remain uncertain.

I do want to acknowledge here a valuable surprise gleaned from my teaching career. In 2005, a group of my students from the past decided to celebrate their 50th eighth-grade graduation from St. Michael School in Shrewsbury, Missouri. They did some "research" on finding their former teachers—and eventually located me, still living and able to celebrate with them. A small group from this class (originally from among my 72 first-graders) continue, to this date, to keep in touch. They take me out to lunch and reminisce about times past. In a very real way, this group of former students is protecting and holding together valuable memories from all our pasts.

Noticing and Responding to Certain Holes in My Life

When I contemplate my poem about the hole (see page 3), I ponder how we humans usually respond to holes which appear in our lives. I know that I, myself, sometimes pretend the hole is not there and try to cover it up. (*I confess that I darned the red sock hole so that it cannot be noticeable to others. Of course, I, myself, know!*)

I am reminded of the era when I first entered the convent (some 60+ years ago). We all wore the traditional long black stockings. A classmate of mine hated to darn; so every time a hole appeared in her stocking, she smeared black shoe polish on her foot to hide the presence of the hole, thus avoiding the need to darn.

Changes In Relationships

Another kind of hole has been appearing in my life more and more frequently—a string of really significant and life-changing events. Three of my dearest, long-term friends have recently died, leaving severe voids which continue to stir my soul more and more each passing day. Each of the three had an advance diagnosis of life-threatening cancer; each lived a few months beyond medical predictions.

My relationship with all three individuals was very different, but each was a long-standing friend. The threads that held us together, while stretched out now so that I can no longer enjoy their physical presence, are still vibrant within me. These are golden threads! I want to replay my memories of each special friend to prevent such golden threads from continuing to wear thin through the coming years (however many!) I still may have ahead here on earth.

I find myself attempting to assure that my relationships with departed friends hold fast. I try to strengthen the threads that bind me to them by keeping in mail contact with their families and other mutual friends. I keep a picture of each of them close at hand so reminders are near. And, perhaps, more significantly, I often call each of them to mind in prayer. I believe they are ever-present in what I call the energy field of cosmic love. Is such a belief too absurd?

Could It Be?

Throughout my earlier years, I held to the traditional understanding of the after-life as a pair of places: one of forever-happiness, and the other a place of eternal pain and punishment. The deeper I now enter into the current scientific and mystical consideration of "evolutionary consciousness" and creation spirituality, the more I think of the *now* as a prelude to death followed by an *after-earth-life* which exists as part of a *yet-to-be-comprehended* field of cosmic energy. We humans are discovering only little by little the realities of our Universe that exist far beyond our planet Earth and what we now see in human and limited ways.

Could it be that, after death, we actually enter into a mystical kind of Universe-community where we not only encounter, in a new way, our Maker/Higher Power, but also experience a different kind of bonding with all those who have, in the past, loved us personally and all those whom we have ever loved? The persons we, still on earth, initially believe we have lost are, perhaps in fact, present beside us, loving us, wishing and willing strength for us, caring for us within the here-on-earth, unimaginable, constant stream of God-love! Couldn't this be so?

Family Threads That Stretch and Strain

As generations in my family expand, I have begun to notice the frequency of my direct contact with them lessens. When my three nieces were small, I saw them often and visited every birthday and holiday. As they turned into young women, married, and began to have children of their own, there seems to be less time for me, their aunt. I keep wondering if all aunties experience some family threads thinning. The threads that kept me very close to my nieces years ago are now stretched out—not broken, but most definitely extended so our interactions are more and more infrequent—or so it seems.

For me, maintaining contact with my nieces and their families is important. This family relationship thread is one I value enormously, and so it is up to *me* to take the initiative in calling them and keeping in touch, however possible. I *purposefully* design opportunities to let them know how important they are to me and how much I love them.

Theme Phrase: "At Your Age . . ."

Having passed my 80th birthday, I began hearing a certain phrase more and more often—"At your age . . ." The remainder of this sentence sometimes continues with a comment such as, "We don't expect you to remember this or that—to be so much on the go—to stay up late—to want to go to the big party." Recently, a surgeon said, "At your age, you are not a candidate for elective surgery."

I admit that, now and then, I hear this phrase with a sense of relief and am glad to be "off the hook." At the same time, this being "at my age" comes to me as a special gift, a grace providing me with extra time, extra space, and opportunity to pursue things I want to do such as the completion of this book.

More and more often, I choose to consider my age in more positive perspective such as how much wiser I am than a decade ago. In addition, I now have more independent time to pray, to reflect, to write, all with the memory and realization that creative writing has been a passion of mine since "way back when."

Attachments To and Detachments From Things

Now and then, I read about elderly and not-so-elderly people who become clutterers or hoarders. Now, in my octogenarian years, I find myself becoming weary of clutter—books, papers, pictures, trinkets. As I ponder what is happening in my mind about *possessions*, I speculate as to whether some innate human characteristic exists that, in preparing us for the end-time, helps us detach.

One day, not too long ago, I opened my clothes closet and was unexpectedly startled by the amount of clothing I found there—a collection of dresses, blouses, skirts, jackets which I wore to present myself to the world as I knew it some years ago. I was astonished as I sensed that my former attachment to favorite articles had disappeared. I began considering, *"What pieces shall I give away? Which to keep?"*

I have a new identity now. In retirement, I am finished needing clothes as some sort of "costume" to present myself. I no longer require the professional woman's façade; and I know for sure that my former desire to "to look attractive" has faded substantially. At long last, I am coming to a deeper comprehension of the difference between "need" and "want"—a basic and emphatic training principle presented to me during my early years in the convent. Armed with this new awareness, it became easy to weed out several outfits for passing on to others who might want, use and enjoy them.

The same kind of phenomenon happened just this past week, when I noted a whole collection of cassette tapes, music I had used when I gave retreats. I needed and wanted to divest of them.

It is remarkable to me that in God's creative design, we humans come to a point of physical wearing out and tiring the closer we come to our appointed death and dying. I no longer have the strength or interest in acquiring more. I long to be rid of "things" that need dusting, moving, keeping track of, stored, protected, and accounted for. Such a wonderful, useful and unexpected grace!

As time unfolds, and I have much more latitude for daily ruminations and reflections, I want to become increasingly aware of which life threads are still vibrant, strong and need my daily attention—and how to let go of those God knows I no longer need as I prepare to let go of *everything*!

I offer two quotations here that I find worthy of deep thought/reflection each time I diminish or add to my set of personal belongings.

> *In the process of letting go you will lose many things from the past, but you will find yourself.*
> - Deepak Chopra

~~~~

> *When I let go of what I am, I become what I might be. When I let go of what I have, I receive what I need.*
> - Tai Te Cheng

Unexpected Grace

I perceive it a special grace to *actually desire* to own less, to have fewer things to maintain— possessions that now seem "in the way" of daily living. This unexpected and welcome course of "letting go" comes hand-in-hand with the daily dwindling of my physical energy . . . not just by coincidence, but by a God-designed facet of the *grace of aging*.

II
My God . . .
Your God . . . Our God

depicting my deepening sense of whom
God is and how and why the relationship
is significant in my daily response to aging

Father David Kraus, OMI (Oblate) had been both my friend and spiritual director over several years. At the close of each spiritual direction session, David would remind me, "Let *your* God be good to you."

I had often wondered why and what David might have intended by the unfamiliar use (at least to me) of the possessive pronoun *your* God. Even though I wondered about it, I never did ask him that question. Alas, David died in 2010. Now I am left to conjecture about David's meaning of the phrase, "*your* God." Now, as I continue the work of composing this text, I have developed my own personal interpretation of David's expression, "*your* God."

My thinking about it goes something like this: everyone has had their individual, personalized introduction to the definition that the English language has wrapped around the concept and word, *God*. Could it be that David was implying that our God, our creator, owns and holds dear-to-heart a divine and uniquely

personalized and loving relationship with *each* created being—animate and inanimate—that He/She has
brought forth into existence?

After all, couldn't it be that God's love for His/Her
off-spring, is not only communitarian (love for all of
creation) but also implies the reality of an entirely
unique and intimate relationship with *each*?

I have come to believe God holds all created beings
in a divine loving and all-encompassing relationship
with the God-self. That being so—then I, you, the
entirety of creation exists, lives, and is ever-embraced
in a specialized stream of love beyond human
description. Thus, the title for this chapter: My
God . . . Your God . . . Our God.

In the months preceding David's stroke and eventual death, I heard him mention his own experience of
new and still-evolving God consciousness. Recently
reflecting on David's deepening grasp of God, the
following thoughts came to me in the early morning
hours. Here are notes from my journal that day
(August 15, 2018):

> *I have come to believe and am moved by*
> *this thought: that the power of God's love*
> *and care for each created being, animate*
> *and inanimate, is unique . . . beyond any-*
> *thing that we humans have been able to*
> *comprehend. At the same time, this crea-*
> *tive love of God unites all beings. May we*

(every being) come, someday, to take in, believe, cling to, and live out the reality of Divine Love's connections between and among us all: my God, your God, our God!

We humans have the faculty of thought, language, and expression to profess our faith in a loving God or, sadly, to deny God. Years ago, I was stunned to hear a close friend exclaim with angry voice, "I don't need a God in my life." I was (and am still) saddened that this friend did not/could not accept the gift I, myself, treasure – belief in a Provident God.

My Childhood Introduction to God

My faith in God began from my mother's prayer and faith example. All through my childhood, even in the hard times of the 1929 Depression, Mother lived, breathed, and spoke these words: "You can't tell me that prayer doesn't make a difference!" My dad became a union organizer and was frequently away. Yet my mother kept-on-keeping-on and prayed us through difficult times and years. She relied on/turned to God with full trust in every moment of crisis. Both parents insisted that I get a Catholic education, elementary and secondary alike.

Undoubtedly, it was Mother's faith-life and my education from the School Sisters of Notre Dame that paved my path to enter the convent after graduation from high school. The influence of my second-grade teacher (Sister Mary Denis, SSND) still remains impactful in my memory. As early as age seven or eight, I wanted to be like Sister Mary Denis—loving, teaching with dedication and commitment, and model of prayer.

The Providence of God: Direction For My Retirement Years

Over the years, I have been a firm believer in the reality and power of what theologians have named the Providence of God. Through this writing, I hope to share the following:

- a powerful insight into how the Providence of God guides me peacefully through each day's events (whether they be happy or challenging)

- a self-revelation that shows me how to live the way to loving as Christ calls us to love—with our *whole heart, whole soul, whole mind*

Our Ever-Providential God

With the frequent practice of mindfulness, I am learning not to spill my thoughts and energies into planning ways to control tomorrow's happenings. In so doing, that is, staying in the present moment—the NOW—I have come to rely more directly on the Providence of this ever-loving God.

I believe that God not only designs each and every second of my own life; but through grace, He/She orchestrates the entire unfolding of events throughout the Universe.

As I age, I notice how many times (too many times?!) I experience nagging incidents of memory lapse. Where did I put my glasses? My keys? What did I do with that stack of mail I just had in my hand? Each significant and insignificant episode of an ordinary day's forgetfulness reminds me of the importance and practicality of keeping focused on the task at hand.

Thus it was that, recently, becoming more and more content/accepting of each day's unfolding, I consciously turned to more mindful thinking throughout each hour—intentionally staying *in the present moment* and keeping my mind focused on the here and now.

My frequent re-reading and reflection on the works of spiritual writers, such as Kathleen Dowling Singh, Grace of Aging and Eckhart Tolle, The Power of Now, opens not only an ever-new awareness of God's grace, but also frees my consciousness of habits that are potential *blocks* to grace.

My God: Up Close and Personal

With more realization and awareness of the world outside and beyond self, I am discovering that my thoughts consciously turn to more expansive thinking throughout the day. While intentionally staying here and now, *in the present moment,* I am more and more realizing a sense of gratitude for the reality of God's personal providence, not only in my own regard, but also in conjunction with all creation.

During an early morning "present moment," God's grace opened to me a fresh perspective of Divine active presence in the Universe surrounding me. In one recent meditation, I became newly conscious of these four attributes of God:

- God is ever **AWARE** of the entire Universe: aware of everything, everyone that will, in time, eventually engage with me in a relationship.

- God **CARES,** at all times, in all circumstances, with an immensity of Divine Love.

- God **PREPARES** those who sincerely call on God for help in engaging each daily task.

- God **REPAIRS** situations stirred up by human error (mine included).

I have discovered by keeping these attributes of God close in mind, any anxiety about making daily choices immediately dissolves. Seeking possible solutions to life's vicissitudes becomes easier. More significantly, I am lifted and freed to respond to daily challenges with full spiritual surrender.

Calling to consciousness this perspective of my God—behold—any emotional turmoil about the day dissolves into a wave of full trust! God's awareness, care, preparing grace, and full repair of any psychological blocks are available *to us all*.

God's Grace:
The Power That Ignites and
Guides Our Daily Choices

The concept of *grace* has enthralled me ever since my childhood years. The <u>Catholic Catechism</u> (1995, page 483) defines grace as a "free and undeserved help that God gives us to respond to the divine call to become children of God and partakers in the life of God."

I have come to believe that the incentive to begin and continue writing this book was the result of God's grace and a two-fold call:

- to set my current life experience of physical aging into perspective with my spiritual growth throughout past years

23

- to offer my story to others as a possible source of insight into their own later years

The Unveiling of Grace

Too often, the presence of a specific grace remains veiled behind the maze of endless thoughts stirring around in our busy brains. We humans (I speak mainly of my own experience) let ourselves become entangled in the busy-ness game I call "*Hurry Up & Get This Problem Solved!*" Each time I rush into the problem-solving process, I miss sensing what theologians call "grace of the moment."

In these, my later years, I actually take more time to pray and reflect. I focus not only on a list of each day's coming significant events, but I also try to give attention to the possible God-connection involved. I believe that it is, indeed, God's grace calling forth my awareness and gratitude for the unfolding of daily choices to be made. Graced choices might be as expansive as my original decision to enter the convent and, eventually, to take on the task of writing this book. They also might be as fleeting as taking the time to admire a flower in the garden and having a beautiful butterfly flutter past just at that particular moment.

I am becoming more and more aware of grace's wonder in both major and minor matters, such as:

- the sudden urge to telephone or send a card to a friend who is ill
- my willingness to offer help with putting a room back in order after the crowd has left
- skipping my favorite TV show (or nap) to attend a last-minute community meeting

In my later years (now nearing 90), I am growing more and more attuned to ponder *daily* grace as preparation for the *final* grace of entry into Eternity.

III
From Center Stage
To Second Balcony,
Near The Exit

emotions evoked when I realize that my professional presence is no longer in demand and my consciousness of how and why in these late years my personal life-values are shifting

Definition of the term "center stage" from Miriam Webster dictionary: middle of the stage, defined role, and privileged position.

Many of us may have had our first "center stage" experience in our mother's womb. A moment when we felt, for the first time, a sense of self-importance. It may be, while still in the womb, we somehow felt the presence of family and friends as they reached out to touch our mother's belly and exclaim how wonderful it was that we were "on the way."

Then, after birth, comes a whole series of our baby performances, one after the other that invited applause—our first smile, our first crawl, our first step, our first word. From what my mother told me and from photos she cherished, I must have *had it all*!

27

Most of us have, perhaps, delighted in moments of center-stage attention and recognition each year as we celebrate our subsequent birthdays.

For many, over our whole-life span, there are moments when we are singularly recognized for achievements or contributions. In those twinklings of special acknowledgment, we are, at the same time, beset by a whole series of expectations—some our own and some in the minds of the public that surrounds us. We may be totally aware these expectations exist, some left to be discovered over our lifetime, and some of which will forever remain hidden.

In most instances, initial expectation is followed by scrutiny of some kind—on our own part, by another person, or from the public in general. The whole phenomenon of recognition, expectation, and public scrutiny are all part of the concept I am naming *"CENTER STAGE."*

Would that we could each recall even one single moment of our actual birth experience! Our birth instant was, after all, our initiation into the human experience of being in center stage. And I cannot help but think of the goodly portion of the world's newborn babies (including ourselves) who so easily capture attention from others, even total strangers passing by along the street or in the store. Tiny babies with their mother are blessed with countless occurrences of center stage as people exclaim, "How cute! "How precious!" and then move on.

Could it not be true that almost every child, including you and me, has, at some time, stood in the middle of an imaginary stage with some imaginary spot light shining on our being? Sometimes the stage may have been real—school plays or concerts for example. Among my childhood memories, the stage was often the bottom of our front steps leading up to my house as my playmates and I acted out spontaneous childish dramas or musical performances.

I choose to temporarily divert focus here to acknowledge and offer a moment of prayer for the unwanted children of the world. For a multitude of serious reasons, many individuals are too-often denied (some throughout their entire lives) the opportunity of being the center of anyone's attention. I pray regularly, and hope that you will too, for these souls in need.

Yet, I, as the first-born in my family, had a goodly share of center stage experience throughout the first five years of my life—until my sister was born.

I honestly don't recall being jealous. I was so happy to have a live-in playmate! As the elder of the two and living together for some thirteen years, I experienced many opportunities to be "the one in charge." Often, both our mother (who worked full-time) and paternal grandmother (who lived with us) would be away, affording me many chances to "take over!" On later occasions, I was even given the major responsibility of navigating my sister and myself down the street unaccompanied by an adult in order to catch the local bus and street-car to meet Mother downtown.

Although I couldn't realize/name it at the time, I was learning the necessity of *personal responsibility*! I do remember sensing the seriousness of the authoritative role entrusted to me. I was "in charge." As adolescent, I was being readied to assume more and more responsibility [*response-ability*] throughout my teens into adulthood.

During my high school years, I felt drawn and specifically called to enter the convent and to become a School Sister of Notre Dame. Following several years of education and training, I became a certified teacher. What more "center stage" role than classroom leader?

Unexpected "Stage Calls"

I had taken my first vows as a School Sister of Notre Dame in 1950 with no thought or intimation that within the next three decades, I would receive several totally unexpected and extraordinary appointments to special roles that would both test and stretch my sense of *"response-ability."*

1962   Sent to pursue full-time study leading to a doctoral degree in French

1965	Appointed Director of the French Department at Notre Dame College in St. Louis
1971	Appointed Acting President of Notre Dame College
1972	Appointed Academic Dean of Notre Dame College
1977	Asked to enter a training program to become a professional group facilitator
1979-81	Elected to the Provincial Council (to replace Sr. Mary Margaret Johanning)
1981	Appointed to be a member of the Revision Committee for our SSND Constitution
1991-99	Elected to the Provincial Council (two consecutive terms)
2009	Invitation to design and conduct a retreat that would combine the SSND Constitution and the Twelve Steps of Alcoholics Anonymous, an idea originated from a previous gathering of "North American Young Sisters"

None of these ministries were sought out by me, but all:

- were asked of me

- gave a direction to each of my days

- kept me in the public eye

- challenged me to keep up-to-date on current information and events

These aspects of role-identity are what I call "center stage" experiences.

Each of my center stage roles bore, with the assignment, a clear job description as a "script" for each day's tasks.

For example, intense preparation for the 2010 retreat consumed nine months of my time and energy (as well as personal prayer and reflection) during composition of the eight separate "talks" in which I sought similarities and possible over-lap of our SSND Constitution <u>You Are Sent</u> (1982) and the Twelve Steps of Alcoholics Anonymous (late 1930's).

The year following the Twelve Step/<u>You Are Sent</u> retreat, my ministry of individual spiritual direction and retreat talks continued. At age 80 plus, I was beginning to experience (more and more frequently!) mid-day fatigue and its effect on the professional quality of my role as spiritual director. Thus came my retirement decision.

Retirement: A New Training Ground For Discovering and Growing In Grace

In early 2012, I announced to my directees that I would no longer be available for consultations. Assisting them as best I could in transferring to another qualified spiritual director, I gave little, if any, forethought to my own transmission into what might be lying just ahead of me as a brand new "retiree."

The written and verbal announcement of my retirement from spiritual direction had much less impact on my psyche than the actuality of no longer having:

- a professional title

- an assigned office space with a plaque on the door announcing my name

- an explicit job description

I had not yet adjusted to, nor embraced, my new identity as "SSND retiree." No longer situated in "center stage," I had, indeed, moved to a "balcony." From this vantage point, I could still see and hear about the all the SSND ministry action and business; but no longer was I directly part of the committees/

groups doing the planning and/or decision-making for our province.

In many ways, the personal decision to retire can feel like a surrender, the notion of which had *never* come easily to me. I had carefully honed my skills to practice, teach and facilitate others in the art of long-range planning—a professional means to take hold of possible and probable outcomes in the future. Suddenly (or so it seemed!), I found myself standing *inside* the formidable "retirement gate."

Help Appears

Kathleen Dowling Singh describes retirement:

> *"Retirement from the pace of midlife places us on utterly new ground. We can feel put out to pasture, naked without the emperor's clothes of a previous position, ringing our hands with nothing enough to do to fill the hours. We can feel unneeded—a difficult experience for many of us whose self-worth depends primarily upon perceiving ourselves to be necessary, indispensable, to others. What a meat hook the word 'indispensable' holds in its guise of goodness."*

-Singh, <u>The Grace of Aging</u>
[Sub-title: *Awaken as You Grow Older*, page 105]

Here I was, nearing age 89, and attempting to describe my own stumbling through these last six years as official "retiree." In hindsight of these immediate past years, I believe I had already passed through at least two "phases" of retirement; and I am only now entering a third phase, including my unexpected discovery of the Singh book just quoted above.

Phase One of Retirement:
A Tsunami-Sort of Endless Questioning

Based on my personal experience, the term "mental tsunami" is not too strong an expression to describe the wheel of psycho-spiritual questions crowding my thoughts in early retirement.

Did I retire too soon? Who am I now? Who do I want to be? What do I want to do? Who do others say that I am now that I no longer have a title? What shall I do with all this time on my hands? Who sees or cares how my days unfold?

During these early retirement years, I tried some volunteer work with the Alzheimer's Association and absolutely loved working beside wonderful men and women who were struggling with their own memory and awareness losses—such difficulties much more severe than any of my own.

Five years later, the Alzheimer's Association made some internal personnel and program changes. The role I had taken on with them was eliminated.

Thus, more questioning about *what next?* and *where?* were added. I found myself watching and waiting for one of our provincial leaders to tap me on the shoulder with a surprising new assignment. Alas, no such request appeared.

Then, the Spirit led me to a deepened personal commitment to daily intensified prayer and meditation. This practice eventually cleared away my sense of anticipating some kind of notable call within the congregation.

Phase Two of Retirement: Learning To Live In The NOW With The Practice of Spiritual Mindfulness

I believe it was through God's urging that I was led to lengthen my daily period of personal prayer, spiritual reading, and contemplation—a special soul-quieting practice readily allowed by retirement's reality.

Singh's book and the writings of Eckhart Tolle continually re-center me in what I had learned sometime in my earlier life as a woman religious—that the experience and practice of mindfulness for short and intermittent times is a sure means of maintaining both serenity and a firmly renewed direction forward,

especially during periods of questioning and/or inde-
cision.

Recently (summer, 2018), being more content and
patiently accepting each moment for what it brings, I
consciously turned to more mindful thinking
throughout the day, staying rooted **in the present
instant** in both thought and focus. This has even had
an amazingly positive impact on dealing with those
inevitable memory lapses I described on page 21.

Over the years along my spiritual development
path, I have heard and read much about the
transcendent practice of mindfulness. Now, in my
life's final phase, I am understanding more than ever
its value as an integral personal exercise.

More importantly, adhering to an everyday-routine
of daily morning prayer lifts and frees me to respond
to any subsequent challenges with an attitude of spiritual surrender. As I said previously, surrender of any
kind had never been a strong suite in my character.

I am learning to *slow down* my habit of spending
thought and energy on trying to control tomorrow's
happenings. By doing so, I remain more firmly rooted
in the present moment—the NOW. It forces me to rely
more directly on God's providence and to trust the
powerful Spirit more readily and directly. The cer-
tainty *is* that this ever-loving God designs each and
every event in my life.

Another startling revelation from Singh's books
brought my attention to the significance of my own

pride and over-active ego—which, in the past few years, has been the source of much soul questioning and unease. Singh has a name for the protruding ego, dubbing our prominent and troublesome habit *"selfing!"* Below is how she describes this human phenomenon:

> *"Most of us have some work to do to enable entry into the opening [of nothingness, the subtle light of emptiness] . . . We can think: how many moments of this day have I spent thinking about 'I' and 'me' and 'mine?' How many moments wondering how each arising circumstance affects me? How many moments resting in the blind conviction that each unexamined, arising belief supports my sense of me? How much clinging and aversion, contraction and lack of ease lie trapped in this tense congestion?"*
>
> -Singh, The Grace of Aging, page 46

I take Singh's questions as a warning, an admonition, and as a healthy gauge/reminder in tracking my own tendency to *"self."* I accept her notion and exposé of selfing as God's grace, a personal response to my frequent prayer: *Jesus, make me meek and humble of heart; make my heart like unto Thine!* After all, wasn't it my selfing whenever I began and carried on my lamentations about no longer occupying center

38

stage? Thus it is that I am marking and naming this next section, *Eclipse of the Ego*.

Phase Three of Retirement:
Eclipse of The Ego

Oxford dictionaries define the word *ego* as "a person's sense of self-esteem or self-importance." The latter connotation is what so often pinches my conscience. Perhaps my mistrust of my own ego stems from past retreats and spiritual readings proselytizing humility as a virtue more desirable than a strong sense of self-importance.

When I use the phrase "ego eclipse" here in conjunction with the third stage of my retirement experience, I am expressing my desire to temper and lessen the frequency of times my inner-antenna are raised to verify who/how many may notice/take interest in my personal projects and undertakings. I realize that solar eclipses are often slow in moving into place before they can actually be noticed. My effort to keep my ego in check may take both commitment and persistence over time.

Thankfully (albeit slowly), I have already begun to experience a new freedom as the result of replacing my focus, concern and fixation about *self* with thoughts of watching and making room for God's own design to transpire each day. In this way, I am *intentionally* making room for my awareness to stretch beyond my personal self-interests, needs and concerns; thus extending my capacity to care for, to be concerned about, and to love others on a substantially deeper level.

At the same time, I am becoming more and more attuned to when I fall back into the habit of selfing. And, thanks to Kathleen Dowling Singh's reminders, I can now more easily cease my selfing before it carries on too long.

In my sincere effort to restrain my selfing habits, I have done some extensive soul-searching about when and how I became so prone to open the door to my own ego-centric thinking, keeping all emphasis on me and mine. All of this has become a definitive awakening about my life-long (off and on) ego-driven habits. I am clearly being led to take serious personal inventory of my many conscious *and* subconscious selfing habits.

I sense that I am being drawn to a response to God described well by Gerald Vann in The Divine Pity: *"You respond to that divine power which will give you the essential integrity without which nothing else is of importance:* **the integrity of self in the infinity of God.**"

Second Balcony: Near The Exit

One could say that the whole retirement experience, especially our post-retirement span of life, have set in motion a metamorphosis of our sense of self. We find ourselves in an unfamiliar, often uncomfortable, *second balcony* of life and action. Now and then we long for the fun and excitement of adventure, but at the same time, we are just as happy to stay at home! The era has arrived when we face friends and acquaintances dying—some unexpectedly. Then, sporadically, thoughts about our own death and dying enter to remind us how near we are to the final exit.

Frequently I find myself identifying with some recently-deceased School Sister of Notre Dame. I wonder how her last moment in life on earth felt. Occasionally, I even have the courage to imagine my own last instant. I desire and hope so much to be surprised when it occurs, but I also want to believe it might be uniquely God-designed in some way, to symbolize the culmination of my personal lifelong relationship with God, who created me.

One recent day, in my sometimes romantic mind, I grasped hold of the notion that I may die soon—perhaps this very year of 2018. Reality soon reminded me that although this thought of dying soon *could* be true, it was more likely only a figment of my fickle, wandering mind. This I know for certain—it behooves me to live each day as if *were* my last – just as I learned from my Catholic school teachers long, long ago.

My number one wish and concern in these late years of life is that I keep my personal relationship with God, my Creator, as center focus of all I undertake and do in my last earthly home.

IV
Learning At Last How To Die

how I came to visualize
the moment of death as
"a free fall" into Cosmic Love

On my 80th birthday, my family threw a grand party. I remember feeling important, honored, and excited, not only by the party's lavishness, but also about the prospect of having an expanse of "retirement" years looming ahead of me. This would be a time to pursue dreams I had, for so long, put on hold. At the same juncture, I found myself appreciating the abundance of life with which I had been gifted.

I thought of the box where my college and university diplomas are stored, along with a multitude of various achievement certificates and a collection of my spiritual journals. Mentally, I celebrated what I then knew of life and made a list of things I yet wanted to experience.

I spent some time revisiting what I had learned from wise and gifted teachers. I had been taught many essential premises intended to support my designated professions. My parents had raised me with what society and religion consider to be acceptable behavior. I continue to learn how to maintain a healthy body. And as years added to my well-earned 80, one question kept nagging at me. *Who teaches us the essentials of dying?*

Sometime after that splendid birthday party, I found myself choosing to initiate a prolonged retreat time, designedly at the Atlantic coast. I wanted to befriend the ocean I once loved but had, since 1996, begun to fear.

This ocean, *these waters*, had years earlier, swallowed the broken fuselage of TWA Flight 800. All passengers and crew rode together, with the wreckage, to certain death. I, myself, had previously safely crossed the Atlantic aboard flight TWA 800 on at least four to six previous occasions. Thus it was that the July 17, 1996 news headlines about TWA 800 riveted my attention—and my imagination—especially about how we humans are so inadequately prepared to face the final journey of dying!

I learned from watching the news that among the passengers aboard this ill-fated Flight 800 were a mother and her two pre-teen daughters. Over and over I replayed that picture in my imagination. I saw and felt the three of them clinging to each other in an embrace the intensity of which they had never felt before. For several years I held that scene wrapped in my own mental label—*horrifying moments ending in unexpected, unprepared death*! I battled with a persistent question: *Does anyone ever intentionally teach us about dying, about how to enter into that moment?*

I began this writing with two objectives in mind:

- to arrive at some personal clarity about how I want to live out these last years of my life

- to share my story and learning with others who may have a desire for clarity about their own dying

Lessons At The Oceanside

St. Joseph Retreat Center is a former 19th century mansion over-looking the Atlantic at Cohasset Bay. Standing or sitting at a Cohasset bayside just south of Boston, one can experience a great span of water from north to south and straight ahead for miles. I spent days on end at the shoreline, trying to imagine the immense depth and width of the Atlantic. Both in reality and in my mind's eye, I saw numberless merchant vessels passing on the far-off horizon. I meditated about the millions of human beings that have come and gone across this expanse of ocean, and I asked myself in wonderment: *How many have met their death in these waters both near and far from land? How many ships have passed this particular spot of earth in the last twenty centuries? How many humans occupy their graves buried beneath these waters?*

I could not help pondering, too, about the underwater world that exists now and in previous times—

deep down in the depths of what is beyond my imagination as my eyes encompassed only a miniscule portion of this vast sea extending across the planet Earth.

The immensity, the mystery, the power of the Atlantic is but a miniature example of the God whom I hoped, during retreat, to ponder and to question. I cannot count the number of hours I sat and stared at this ocean, a real but minimal metaphor of God—the Power and Love in Whom I fully believed.

Only a week or so after my arrival at St. Joseph, I heard a radio weather report warning of an approaching storm. An early nor'easter was headed this way with high wind and possible heavy snow. The trees were still in leaf; so heavy snow and strong winds meant a highly feasible power-outage. With only two of us now in residence at this huge house and the owners away for the week-end, I began to worry.

Just as I was about to prepare my small supper in the microwave, my fears came to fruition, and the power went down. I could hear the pounding of waves just below my window. As the wind picked up, the temperature both inside and outside dropped. With no light or electricity, I decided going to bed might help keep me warm. I wondered about possible wind damage. What to do?

As I lay in the dark, I prayed that somehow I could keep fear at bay. I began to think of the Flight 800 mother and her two daughters, and the panic that must have engulfed them in their last hour aboard the plane. An image unexpectedly came to me of that mother and her two daughters wrapped together in a group hug as they fell into the immensity of the ocean. With that vision, in *that moment*, I learned and came to believe this about dying:

DEATH IS LIKE A FREE-FALL INTO THE IMMENSITY OF PURE LOVE!
♥

During their moments of terror, these three family members must have experienced, in that final hug, the *greatest* expression of love they had ever known from/through/with each other. This realization about "a free fall into love's immensity," was my first memorable learning about how to die!

Ever since my spiritual vision that stormy night, I contemplate my eventual death as a "free fall" into God who, according to my belief, ___IS LOVE___! With this perspective, how on earth can I possibly be fearful of that last moment of life-as-I-have-known-it-until-now?

Soon after the storm and my vision of the mother with her daughters, I wanted to know about them: their names, their home, etc. After electrical power had been restored, I used the computer to research the actual date of the TWA 800 disaster and the names of the mother and her daughters. To my astonishment

47

and delight, I found something else to confirm the clarity of my image of the three in a final embrace.

Sometime shortly after their death, their husband/father commissioned a statue of the three to be made and erected in their home town. The statue portrays exactly what I had imagined—*all three in a grand embrace*! The news article included a picture of the statue, clearly showing the detail of this cherished family trio, gathered together as one with arms about each other in a magnificent gesture of love connection.

Receiving this unmistakable message from God has undoubtedly been one of the most powerful, moving and valuable spiritual experiences of my life.

More Yet To Be Learned

When it was time to leave Cohasset after my first startling lesson about dying, another necessary lesson was about to be revealed.

A dear and long-time friend, Hank by name, came to pick me up from the retreat center and drive me to his family's home in New Hampshire for a week-end visit. Neither Hank nor his family nor I knew this visit was prelude to my next installment in learning how to die. The following spring, I was to be cast into an intense and long-lasting "internship" dealing with death and dying.

Seven months following my visit with Hank and his family, he was diagnosed with pancreatic cancer. He passed on just six-months later (November 2012).

Around the same time, another close friend, Ann, suffered the last stages of stomach cancer and died (September 2012) just two months prior to Hank.

Two other friends are, at the time of this writing (early 2013), living the life we can designate only as "chemo patients." And there is a fifth person, too, a former eighth-grade classmate, who (by choice) is in the dying process without chemo.

Why, I asked time and time again, *have all these death and dying events been unfolding around me?* Other octogenarians soon answered my question with an emphatic declaration, "That's what you can expect after you have turned 80!"

V
Encountering Life's Unexpected Turbulence

seeking grace to "see it through"

On December 16, 2018, I wrote in my personal journal:

> *Forty-eight hours ago I was witness to my sister's final breath following her transfer from St. Mary's Hospital to DeGreef Hospice House.*

My three nieces and I had spent the previous ten days experiencing the gradual letting go of someone dearly loved. For me, this was a painful period of tearing away my 85-year-long relationship with my "little sister." I found myself, an 89-year-old nun, whining to my God, *I don't want this to be so! Not now; it's Christmas time!*

The newness, agony and acuity of this slow-moving separation stretched out for almost a full week as we, the family, prepared for the wake and planned the funeral Mass. How many parents, spouses, children have experienced this same kind of bonded relationship being torn asunder by the death of a loved one? Nearly everyone goes through it at some point in their life. Certainly in almost every such encounter, inside is a painful longing for life to return to "normal."

Some days later, I experienced grace with an unexpected and clear realization which somehow broke through in the midst of my mental tangle of worry and puzzlement about my present life situation. I was, at last, able to consent to the loss of my sister.

Consent: A Step Beyond Surrender

My one and only sister lay dying this pre-Christmas December morning. I believe I had spiritually moved beyond resistance to a deep and profound acceptance of the actually-losing-her reality. As I saw and heard her tossing and moaning, I found myself balking at my own powerlessness to be of help or offer words of meaningful comfort. I realized, then, that I had little choice other than surrendering her to God's care. But I hadn't yet *consented* to her dying, to my own loss of her physical presence, her smile, her voice.

Grief grew, receded, and grew again like an endless storm . . . sometimes in full rage, sometimes moving away only to return, setting me again into unbridled wrath. I cry out: "I miss you!" I scream at my sister—then the tears come, softening and melting me into a new kind of humility.

I share with you a quote from my personal journal of December 17, 2018 two days following her actual death:

> *Surrender is passive thinking, a simple "let it be so!" Consent is my full handing over, in mind and heart, to the divine scheme of things . . . my relaxing into the full mystery of her life and her own life's surrender in a way that intertwines with my own and letting be what is. Letting her "be"—not gone from my life, but now a newly-spirited part of my life.*
>
> *Memories remain of how we were intertwined with how we are now: still blood-sisters, still daughters of the same parents, still loving the living of our joint family. My consent to how-things-are-between-us at this moment includes the reality of sharp, now-and-then waves of grief.*

Grief Revisited

Just before the spring's arrival in 2019, I attended a funeral for one of my small-community SSND's brother. The funeral liturgy that day was exceptionally beautiful; yet the experience opened within me once more an invasive reality of loss and pain. Grief's weight that day came over my being like a molasses waterfall—heavy and ever-so-slowly enveloping all of my senses.

At this writing, I have an intuition that my grief over the loss of my sister will become a frequent visitor . . . coming, going away for a while, then returning . . . often when I least expect it . . . oozing into my consciousness, sometimes quietly, sometimes like a surgeon's scalpel.

Tools For Turbulent Times

At this late time in my life—at this advanced age—in times of severe turbulence, I know my own inadequacies. I act instinctively by *turning to my God*! I wrote earlier in this book about my beliefs in God's own *awareness*, not only of all that is occurring in my life, but in the wideness of God's *care*, not only for me, but for all persons that live and have lived.

During my times of pain, loss and powerlessness, I believe it is God alone who encases the total picture in some Divine Awareness and Mercy lying far beyond my own limited comprehension. At the same time, I do believe in the infinite expanse of God's power! Thus, *turning to God* is "Tool #1" for me to emotionally survive life's turbulent times!

"Tool #2" which I have found helpful and powerful—*situating the story within my life's history*. I need to intentionally station the current burdensome event within the recent timeline of my personal spiritual development.

To help me identify this, I checked back in my journal. What had been happening in my spiritual life just before my sister's last stage of illness on-set?

I believe *God's working within me* is ongoing in certitude—that is, not outside of and not disconnected from God's consistent flow of grace tuning my spirit.

The seriousness and finality of my sister's illness became most evident the day after Thanksgiving 2018. Now, as I check my spiritual journal from that time, I find such entries in my own handwriting:

> *10/29 I ask for the graces of generosity and humility.*

> *10/30 Today, I am willing to be WHO and HOW I am in Your sight.*

> *11/02 You hold me in Your hand . . . You care for all . . . You envelop me and the Universe in LOVE . . . in CARE.*

> *11/08 I watch the leaves fall from the tree that had been dressed in full beauty just a few days ago...the leaves seem to tremble before letting go. I want to surrender, handing over my body and spirit to YOUR CARE!*

11/11 SURRENDER = impermanence of life and control.

I trust that the reader of this text can now understand, with me, how my spiritual expansion in the weeks before my sister's final illness came to be such a consolation for what was to follow. Another key facet is how valuable the practice of journaling can be.

VI
And Now The End Is Near

bringing the book to closure
synonymous with what's happening
for me physically and spiritually

I borrow this phrase, "the end is near," from a song popularized by Frank Sinatra in 1969 (lyrics by Paul Anka). The title of the song is *My Way* with a repetitious chorus line declaring, "I did it myyyy way!"

I never considered the writing of my book as something I did "my way." Rather, I experienced this whole process as an alluring invitation to record my personal observations and learnings about human aging. My desire is to offer the book as a "gift" to others who are entering their octogenarian years and experiencing the momentous changes that occur within, without, and around the human being we call *self* in the latter years of life. I do so in the belief that my insights may help strengthen someone's faith in God and/or assist in making new life choices. Above all, I hope to glorify God in the realization of Spirit's never-ending gift of grace galore each day we inhabit this earth. I do not want or need to declare that I did it all *my way* but only rather that (with God's help) *I DID IT*!

The long-in-the-making of this manuscript is nearing its own end. My body and mind are becoming weary of all the preparatory tasks—resource reading and referencing, note-taking, note organization, plus adequate and easily accessed storage of materials.

I had begun this work in 2014 in a formal education class offered at one of the local community colleges entitled "Creative Writing." My original outline (as required by the instructor) had listed ten chapters; but now, my weary psyche has decided *enough is enough*! My current mid-day thought patterns keep crying out to me, *be done with it!* And so, I offer this text to you, dear friends, as it is . . . a text perhaps yet needing to be edited, reformatted, whatever. Yet, here it is—AS IT IS!

> *Our destiny is to go beyond everything, to leave everything, to press forward to the End and find in the End our beginning, the ever new beginning that has no end.*
> - Thomas Merton

As I bring this writing adventure to a close after five years, I find myself both shocked and embarrassed that after a brief editing and rearranging of texts, I am coming up with fewer than 100 pages. I recognize, only now, how many times I have written and rewritten the same sections more than once. Perhaps I needed to keep writing the same things over and over again to drive home *to myself* the messages I was trying to convey?!

Can it be that during those five years when I so often made conversational reference to "my book," that now, lo and behold, I have only a "booklet?" Booklet is defined by Google as a small, thin book with a paper cover. This definition surely fits the document you, the reader, are now holding in your hand. Whatever its physical dimension, book or booklet, it still bears five years of concentrated thought, prayer, energy, trial and persistence.

There were days during the on-going creation of these chapters that my eyes dimmed and my energies lagged—even more so when I allowed my mind to wander and fret about my own aging. I would began to think about bringing this work to a close *ASAP*— off and on considering the possibility of simply quitting and letting it end wherever I happened to be on that given date and time. During these intervals, right then and there I would turn to prayer; and in just a moment or so, I would quickly sense that quitting now was not an acceptable choice.

In the Sunday homily on July 15, 2018, a call within me awakened my spirit and moved me on. The liturgical celebrant that day spoke of our often childish habit of asking, "Why?"

Immediately, my mind queried, *why should I continue working on the book*?! Yet, because of that day's morning quiet prayer time (where I happened to hatch new ideas for phrasing and new concepts to add to the text), I straightaway knew the answer to my *why* question—***THIS BOOK IS MY CALLING!***

Each day, I am reaching closer to my 90's, which will actually be my *one hundredth* decade!!! Death may be soon, even though not yet in view. I chose to continue the book, and to follow God, my creator/ director and the *true* author of this work. As I continue seeking solutions to life's daily challenges and vicissitudes, keeping the reality of God's nearness in mind immediately dissolves any anxiety I may feel about making both significant and insignificant daily choices.

Each day, time becomes more precious, vitally of essence. This very morning, I awakened and turned over slowly, only to sense that my legs and arms felt sluggish, tingling, and quite limp. I am not sure in what position I had been sleeping, but the experience of numbness, sleeping arms and legs frightened me. *Am I having a stroke?* was my first thought. I began to stretch my extremities, and gradually, all began to feel normal. While I was relieved no sign of stroke truly existed, the whole experience underscored the reality of my daily aging process.

For the rest of this morning, after fully awakening from the sleeping-appendages episode, I sensed an urgency to start working, more intensely and steadily, on writing and bringing my book project to a close. With that 90th birthday looming close, there exists a mysterious count-down of the days, months, years I will remain living and healthy enough to write and pursue other projects. Time ticks louder each day for this octogenarian!

Even as my physical energies wane and body parts are breaking down, God's wondrous grace continues to abound in unexpected respects. I am both surprised and astonished at this particular grace phenomenon— how a multitude of physical diminishments so easily open a latch allowing long-term attachments to people, places and *favorite things* to float easily away.

Precisely because I no longer have energy to care for books, pictures, souvenirs and other possessions, or to contact/visit long-term friends, I am learning to value more highly the gift of quiet moments, free afternoons for naps, peace-filled evenings. I now find myself looking forward to the day (coming quickly!) when I can dispose of all the scribbled notes I have collected in the five-year process of writing this book. What a freedom is on its way! What a time of grace is yet to emerge!

Epilogue

I sincerely hope something you have read here will be of help in your own personal journey. This I firmly believe—that my daily experience and all those I've shared here with you are, in reality, a miniscule element in the world's turning.

Our Universe is a complex cosmos, the breadth of which we can *never even begin* to comprehend. I leave you with the challenge to remain in the wonder of it all as we allow ourselves to ponder our existence with "a grain of salt, a heart full of gratitude, and a truckload of humor."[1]

---

[1] Source of quote unknown

Appendix

Reflection Questions

I *Thinning of Threads and Starkness of Holes*
"Teachment" is the word I learned to name those life experiences which etch significant marks in my memory and serve as a guide to render various future decisions.

Name some significant teachments from your own life.

Recall any events that may have changed and/or challenged your concept of your "professional identity." Examine how you responded to such a change and/or challenge.

From your memory of that particular professional identity, what can you recollect with a sense of pride?

What part of your professional identity was a special challenge?

II *My God ... Your God ... Our God*
Describe in a short paragraph your image of "YOUR GOD."

When, where and how do you believe this impression originally came to you?

What is your own understanding of grace?

What would you name as one of the most significant graces God has bestowed on you most recently?

**III   From Center Stage To
Second Balcony Near The Exit**
What has been your own experience of being in "center stage?"

Describe your stepping away from "center stage" and the feelings and sentiments you recognized at that time.

Have you undergone an official "retirement?" From what? Describe (a) how the early stage of retirement felt, and (b) some of your spiritual awakenings during this phase.

What mental or spiritual practices helped you adjust to being retired?

After reading pages 39-40 (Eclipse of the Ego) how would you describe the state or changing state of your own ego?

IV   Learning At Last How To Die

Have you given any thought to what you can imagine about the human experience of dying?

Express what you believe about the death experience.

What might you hope and pray about your last year of life?

V   Encountering Life's Unexpected Turbulence

Take time to discover what mental/spiritual practices work best for you in times of turbulence in your life:

- *prayer, turning it over to God*
- *practice of spiritual mindfulness*
- *talking it over with a friend or counselor*
- *discovering new ways to elicit peace of mind*

VI   And Now The End Is Near

Looking over the immediate past decade of your life, what do you believe is the most significant task God has laid before you? Elaborate on that thought in terms of how it has affected you.

How do you now feel, thus far, about your fulfillment of that task?

Suggested Readings

Avis Clenenden, <u>Spirituality in Depth</u>, Cheron Publications, 2002

Ilia Delio, <u>The Emergent Christ: Exploring the Meaning of Catholic in Evolutionary Universe</u>, Orbis Books, 2011

Alexander Eben, <u>Proof of Heaven: A Neurosurgeon's Journey Into the Afterlife</u>, Simon and Schuster, 2012

Esther Luttsell, <u>Between Heaven and Earth: Proof Beyond Doubt That Life and Love Are Eternal</u>, Wild Rose Press, 2013

Richard Rohr, <u>Falling Upward: A Spirituality for the Two Halves of Life</u>, Jossey Bass, 2011

Kathleen Dowling Singh, <u>The Grace in Aging</u>, Wisdom Publications, 2014

Kathleen Dowling Singh, <u>The Grace in Dying</u>, Harper Collins, 1998

Marsha Sinetar, <u>Don't Call Me Old, I'm Just Awakening!</u>, Paulist Press, 2002

Echart Tolle, <u>The Power of Now</u>, New World Library, 1999